I have been looking for a book like this that would help with the honor and challenges of grand parenting. I am not aware of anything on "GrandFathering" in the bookstores or libraries. Dan is a godly friend who loves people and especially his family. Thank you Dan, you nailed it!

    – Harold Finch, Ed. D; NASA scientist, business founder, educator and lay missionary

Dan Erickson speaks to grandfathers from the perspective of his own personal journey as a grandfather. His brilliant focus on two key principles—your talk talks and your walk talks, but your walk talks louder than your talk talks, and you can't give what you don't have—frame practical applications of intentionality we all need to examine more carefully. Grandfathering: Live to Leave a Legacy will give you invaluable tools for your grandfathering toolbox—if you're serious about living a legacy that matters.

    – Cavin Harper, Courageous Grandparenting

Dan's book on GrandFathering comes at a time when the historical family unit is in serious decline. As the family goes... so goes a nation. Grandfathers play a unique role in the development of kids (and adults) that can be filled by no other. Dan's book is a call to men (Grandfathers) to become purposeful and strategic in building those most special relationships... relationships that will positively impact lives and extend into eternity.

    – Greg Quakenbush, Regional Sales Manager

GrandFathering is a must read for anyone who wants to be a "great" grandfather to his grandchildren. Dr. Erickson clearly identifies the essential characteristics of grandfathers who inspire their grandchildren and leave a legacy of which anyone would be proud. He has challenged all of us to intentionally and thoughtfully demonstrate for our grandchildren the love of Christ and how to trust him in all things.

– Dr. Jim Guth, Regional Director for the Billy Graham Evangelistic Association

This is truly a book for our time. When so few family units are still intact, knowing how to be a better Grandfather is absolutely imperative. Today's children need the influence that a good Grandfather can bring. I've known "Dr. Dan" for many years and watched him transition from a good father to a great Grandfather. Does he have all the answers? No, but I know he lives what he teaches, and he's teaching from experience. We can all become better Grandfathers by reading and applying the principles shared in this book. Thanks Dan for writing this book.

– Mike Jackson, Sales Representative

I have known and observed Dr. Dan Erickson as a man, husband, father, grandfather and ministry leader for nearly two decades. He is a man who God has entrusted with rich principles for living. This work is far more than just another book on Grandfathering - it is a training manual for grandfathers of all ages. Whether your grandchildren are infants, toddlers, children, young adults or out of your house, reading and using the concepts from Dan will be one the greatest gifts you can give your children, grandchildren and generations yet to be born.

– Ray Morgan, Insurance Broker, Retired

I have read many books in my life but I never read a book more relevant to where I am in my life right now. My three grandsons are going to benefit from what I have learned from this informative and practical book. I recommend it to any grandfather who wants to effectively "live a life and leave a legacy."
– Daryel Erickson, Missionary

Dan Erickson has knocked it out of the park with his latest book, GrandFathering: Live to Leave a Legacy. This is more than a "Must Read" for Grandfathers and future grandfathers. This is a much-needed resource for men to "soak in" and "live out." Dan gives us timeless principles with clear and simple applications to improve the game of any grandfather. This Book does not need to be on every bookshelf – it needs to be in the hands of every Grandfather!
– Dr. Chuck Stecker – President, A Chosen Generation/Center for InterGenerational Ministry

A book for grandfathers WOW…. How overdue. Whether you're in your 40's, 50's or 60's or older get down on the floor and play with your youngsters. You'll have the most fun and your grandchildren will never forget.
– Gary Mandernach, Business Owner

GRANDFATHERING
Live to Leave a Legacy

Dr. Dan Erickson

credo
house publishers

Grandfathering: Live to Leave a Legacy

Copyright © 2014 Dan Erickson

Published by Credo House Publishers,
a division of Credo Communications, LLC, Grand Rapids, Michigan.
www.credohousepublishers.com

ISBN: 978-1-625860-17-0

Printed in the United States of America
First edition

Contents

Section 1
Living a Legacy

Section 2
Leaving a Legacy

Acknowledgments

I want to express my appreciation most of all to my seven grandchildren – Gabby, Kayla, Alex, Dylan, Bella, Hallie and Danny – for teaching me how to be a grandfather and allowing me to share the lessons I have learned.

Thank you Cathy for being a godly grandmother. You have set the standard I strive for as a husband, father and grandfather.

I wasn't always there for my children, Shannon and Doug. Thank you both for my beautiful grandchildren and the opportunity for a do-over. I appreciate your mates Rusty and Ginny for having patience with me as I discover what it means to be their friend.

Thanks to those who give insights in the book from their personal testimonies to what they have learned and experienced with their grandfather.

Someone once said,
"Had I known grandkids were so much fun,
I would have had them first."

A grandfather once wrote:
"For I know the plans I have for you,' declares the Lord,
plans to prosper you and not to harm you,
plans to give you hope and a future."
(Jeremiah 29:11 – NIV)

I pray that will be the goal of every grandfather.

Preface
By First Granddaughter Gabby, God's very best!

What my grandfather means to me is something that can only be described through the little moments. It can be seen through the way he always "let's" me win at Scrabble, in the way he reaches over and eats the food off our plates when he thinks we're finished, in the way he can simultaneously watch a muted USC game on the television and talk to us about how we're liking our classes at school.

It can be seen in the way he always shows up to our plays or baseball games, wholeheartedly being supportive but occasionally talking in a volume that he believes quiet, but is still over heard by those around us.

My earliest remembrance of my grandfather is when I was sitting in the backseat of the car, and I told him that I loved him this much. I spread my arms out as wide as they could go to illustrate the abundance of my love for him. Whether this is an actual memory or my mind's reconstruction of a story told to me many times I'm not sure. Either way I can still say with widespread arms that I love my grandfather this much.

It's a testament to his character and involvement in my life that I can say with such honesty that my grandfather is one of the greatest men I have ever known. As such, the importance of this book is insurmountable to all grandfathers, providing a guide to loving your grandchildren and showing this love through simple actions.

Being a grandfather is different than any other role, and its uniqueness provides uncharted territory and a new challenge for any man blessed with grandchildren. Growing up, my grandfather (the esteemed author of this extremely amazing book) played a very active part in my childhood; a part which I believe helped make me become who I am today. His encouragement and confidence in my ability to be 'God's best' was a constant reminder that I was special not only in the eyes of my grandfather, but also in the eyes of God. I am so grateful that God has given me such a loving, generous, and sometimes embarrassingly honest grandfather, and I have full confidence that this book will help any grandfather strengthen their relationships both with their grandchildren and with God.

Sincerely, Gabby

The Grandfather's Prayer

*"I will come and proclaim your mighty acts, O Sovereign Lord;
I will proclaim your righteousness, yours alone.*

*Since my youth, O God, you have taught me;
and to this day I declare your marvelous deeds.*

*Even when I am old and gray, do not forsake me, O God;
til I declare your powers to the next generation;
your might to all who are to come."*
(King David – Psalm 71:16-18 NIV)

The Heart of the Author
Papa Dan

God loves grandfathers! You may feel like you are the best grandfather or the worst. Most of us aren't either. This book is designed for you to help yourself and others. It will help you become who God wants you to become. Grandfathering was a "Do-Over" for me. Maybe it will be for you also.

I don't suggest you read this book all at once. The truth can be overwhelming. Read a chapter, and then wait and mediate on what God is trying to show you. Some principles will be repeated throughout the book. If you are anything like me, you won't get things that might apply to your life the first time.

God loves to repeat things, too.

I hope you will enjoy the truths God showed me over the past 19 years, both through personal experience and from His word. I promise I will not preach at you. Remember, you can be God's best; now go be who you are. Become the best grandfather your grandchildren need and who God has designed you to become.

I encourage you to pray this prayer from an old song I used to sing in my dad's church.

Sweet Holy Spirit, sweet heavenly dove,
Stay right here with us, filling us with your love.
And for these blessings we lift our hearts in praise;
without a doubt we'll know that we have been revived,
when we shall leave this place.

Your Friend and Fellow Grandpa,
Dr. Dan Erickson
CSL, People Matter Ministries

Introduction
A Fresh Start

Real-Life
Real-Life Moment of Destiny

"Grandchildren are the crown of an old man..."
(Proverbs 17:6)

I walked into the living room, looked into the sweet eyes of my daughter Shannon, and instantly she began to cry.

She seemed overcome with fear and her eyes gazed at the floor while tears streaked her cheeks. Through sobs, she said, "Dad, I'm pregnant."

My wife Cathy sat beside me as Shannon's sobs broke my heavy silence. I sat there bewildered as the waterfall of thoughts rushed through my head. My daughter had recently graduated high school and was beginning her walk into adulthood. Travel weary, I had just returned from training in Denver, after recently being appointed as Promise Keeper's regional director for the Northwest. I was just 44 years old, and a pregnant teenager was not part of my five-year plan.

Thankfully, my heavenly Father quieted this inner turmoil and not a word of it was breathed. In a still small voice he spoke to my sprit: "Tell Shannon what I have told you time after time. This is part of my plan for her life and I am with her. As well, this child will usher in the beginning of a new and rewarding life for you and Cathy."

It must have been an extended time, because my wife, Cathy, shook me out of my bewilderment when she said, "Say something!" I expressed to Shannon our commitment to be there for her and her baby. I told her, *"There was a God in heaven who loved her unconditionally and there was a dad on earth who did too."*

God was right! It began a journey of grandfathering that changed my life. I have to admit that I was, like many of you, a preoccupied father. I struggled with my own insecurities, seeking to please others, and I often lost sight of those people in my life that really mattered most. I often allowed the "whats" in my life to determine my identity and significance which affected how I related with the "whos" in my life; my wife and children and now grandchildren. In many ways, through my grandchildren, I got a "do-over, a fresh start."

Shannon gave birth to our first grandchild, Gabrielle, who we affectionately call "Gabby." She is now 19 years old, going on 25, and working her way through college.

In our book "God Loves Do Overs!" published in 2009, my daughter Shannon wrote,

"This was a very painful time in my life, and I was overwhelmed by the pain of disappointing my parents, of not having a father for my baby, of losing some of my friends, and of a major life-change that I wasn't ready for. I could have wallowed in self-pity and even given up hope that things would never be normal for me, but I decided to wait for something extraordinary to happen."

Something extraordinary did happen. God allowed Cathy and I to become part of a moment in their destinies. That moment in

1994 could have gone quite differently. I realize now that God was testing me for he already knew what he was going to do. It really is so true that God never says "Oops!" He was giving me a fresh start; he was giving me a do-over.

Shannon would get a do-over too. She married a wonderful man who adopted Gabby, and they gave me four more grandchildren. My younger son, Doug, found a beautiful lady and gave me two more. God has blessed me with a full quiver. My God, my wife of 43 years, my two kids, and my seven grandchildren are the loves of my life. Apart from God and them I am nothing.

Family is the true expression of the heart of the Father.

I have determined in my heart and spirit, with the help of God Almighty that I will live a life that will leave a legacy, one that will echo now and for eternity. I am going to leave my grandfathering legacy through the life that I live, and I am going to imagine the possibilities!

You can too! Today can be the beginning of the rest of your life.

Maybe you can identify with me; you also need a do-over. The purpose of this book is simple: I want to stir up and call out of every grandfather the belief that they can make a difference, that they can leave a legacy through grandfathering.

The cool part of being a grandfather
is not so much about the destination but the journey.
It finds its best legacy when it is lived out in our lives.

What my education and occupations could not teach me, I

have learned from my wife; children and grandchildren over the last many years. I am continuing to learn how to be a grandfather that is leaving a legacy now and for eternity.

We should not fear failure.
We should fear that we would spend our lives succeeding
at what really does not matter.

The following are keys I have learned over the last 19 years to help unlock my grandchildren's heart and my legacy.

My hope and prayer is that they will help you too.

The Legacy Question

If you knew you could become a grandfather who would intentionally commit to living and leaving a Godly legacy to your wife, children and grandchildren – one that would echo now and for eternity – would you become that kind of grandfather?

Grandfathering is not so much about doing but becoming.
The doing leaks out!

Consider these as absolutes. I do!

As a grandfather…

- You can only live out in your life or family what you have first learned and applied yourself.

- You can only give to your family what you have first possessed for yourself.

- You will only lead your family where you are first willing to go.

- You will only see whom you care about and care about whom you see.

- You can only reproduce in your life and family who you choose to become.

Pray for your children and grandchildren every day.
Name them by name.
It is the next best thing as being there.

SECTION 1:

Living a Legacy
for
Your Grandchildren

When you are with your grandchildren,
Be there. Be engaged.
They will notice the difference.

Chapter 1
A Life That Transforms

I hope you will agree with me that being a grandfather is not so much about making a legacy for us but about living a legacy for our grandchildren. The ultimate goal for us as grandfathers is to live a life that serves to transform our decedents into the men and women God wants them to become.

The ultimate question for us is,
Am I part of the transformational solution
or part of the problem?

I'm not sure how that may look from your vantage point. I don't walk in your shoes. I have to be honest that as my grandchildren are growing up, I have as many questions as I do answers. Maybe we can discover the answers together. I will attempt to give you some insights that God has shown me and my family over the years in which I have had the privilege of being called "Papa Dan."

I will attempt over the next few chapters to help you discover how you can help your grandchildren become transformed and at the same time live and leave a legacy that echoes now and for eternity.

I will urge you to consider specific principles and practices in the coming pages, but here is the key to the whole book: If you are going to become a transforming grandfather, you will need to be transformed. In other words, if you want to have meaningful impact on your grandchildren's lives and help them become God's best, you will have to search your soul and allow God to have meaningful impact on your life.

I also will ask you many questions in the coming pages. But the ultimate questions are these:

What kind of legacy are you living now, and
what kind of legacy do you hope to leave?

Warning: This chapter is the longest in the book because it sets everything up. The others are much shorter. As I have gotten older shorter is better. So hang in there!

Let's start with some basics I learn over the years. God gives each of us:

Eyes that see;
Ears that hear;
A heart that feels;

A mind that reveals;
Words that express;
Feet that walk;
Hands that hold; and a
Life to be transformed.

Eyes that See

First you have to see them.

I have to admit I struggled as a dad. So I made a decision that I was going to be a better grandfather than I was a dad. I saw my grandchildren, in many ways, as a do-over! I spent much of my life trying to change the world around me but lost sight that those in my own home were not getting my very best.

My own grandfathers didn't teach me about the importance of living in order that I might leave a legacy. I think I loved my grandfathers because I was supposed to. I really never knew them. I don't even think they ever really saw me. I am not trying to be critical. My family had five kids, so we were like a moving target. I don't remember ever having a meaningful conversation. I think this left a grandfather-shaped vacuum in my heart. My children would probably say the same about my dad, their grandfather. He could not give what he had never received for himself. I believe he never really knew he needed to be an engaging grandfather. No one encouraged him to think differently as I am attempting to do for you.

How is your vision? Is it 20/20?

When my grandchildren come over, I have made it a habit to stop what I am doing, look into their eyes, tell them I love them and give them a hug and a kiss on the forehead. When your grandchildren come by do you go see them?

What or who is taking your focus? Do you look up from your game or newspapers to give them a glancing look but never really see or engage them?

"Eyes to see" mean you get engaged, you make eye contact.

I don't know what "getting engaged" means to you, but for me it involves all my senses. It is amazing what you can learn about them and about you.

Seeing them leads to believing in them.

I invented a creature called the "The Claw." When the grandchildren come to the house, the younger ones immediately look for a place where they can hide. When I find them I start with the neck, then move down to the chest onto the ribs, and finally down to the knees. By this time they are laughing hysterically. (It only works on 9-years-olds and below.) For me it has been a great way of engaging them right when they come in the door. (Important: Give them time to hide.)

Bottom line: invent ways that they see you and you see them. Be creative!

If they can't see you, you won't see them.
Do you become invisible?

Ears that Hear

God intentionally gave us two ears and one mouth,
which do you think He wants us to use the most?

Sit back in your easy chair, and what do you hear? What are your grandchildren saying? What are they asking you? It is hard to listen to the game, read a newspaper and pay the bills while trying to listen to them, read their response and engage in a loving and caring way. Do they get quiet when you come into the room? Do you encourage appropriate noise or do you flee when they cause a ruckus. Do they flee from you? Do you ask questions, or do you grow quiet?

Silence is not golden.

Earn the right to speak into their lives. When you speak to them, is it more of an interruption? Do you have the ears to hear or do you become hard of hearing or maybe even deaf?

I have sought to discover when each of my grandchildren opens up the most. If it is in the car, I take a lot of car rides. If it is working outside, I find jobs for them to do with me. (A little payment for these jobs helps.) Find the place where they talk and exploit it. Earn the right to be heard by listening.

Here are some places where my grandchildren open up the most.

Gabby – Going out to lunch or dinner, or riding in a car (must be in the front seat).

Kayla – Shopping, riding in a car or going out on a grandpa date (must buy).

Alex – Working with me (pay helps) and playing with dog or sports (in that order).

Dylan – Counting money or playing dominos (helps with math skills and the winner gets $1).

Bella – Loves to read to me and play in the park (mostly on the monkey bars).

Hallie – Loves the "The Claw" tickling her, and playing with her dolls (her favorite doll is Madison).

Danny – I get my exercise keeping up with him. Loves to laugh, talk and play with Legos. (He's all boy).

The key is get to know them.
Allow them to make a lot of joyful noise,
because their silence is not golden.

A Heart that Feels

When I say a heart to feel it really means to feel their pain, their needs, their desires, their fears, their aspirations. How are you feeling with your heart? If you are one of those guys who say you are not the feeling kind, let me suggest something for you: "Get over it!"

Let what you feel from your heart determine what you say!

One of my granddaughters decided to try out for a part in a play. I told her I would pray for her. So I did right then. After the tryout I asked her if she got the part. She said with sadness in her voice that she did not get the part but it was cool to hear her say at the end, "It just wasn't God's will for me at this time. I will keep trying." I was so proud of her. The best thing I could say was nothing. A smile and a hug sometimes speak louder than words.

May I suggest a few responses to situations in our grandchildren's lives?

- When they are sad, feel their disappointments or fear. Kids can get depressed too.

Our response: It won't be easy, but don't try to fix it. Just listen, pray to yourself or with them – and hugs really help.

- When they are being disobedient and won't obey. (We know this seldom happens.)

Our response: If they have parents around pray (not out loud) and let them deal with it.

I'm not a big fan of grandparents using physical punishment. Be creative! Be calm! When you lose your temper you lose. Loving discipline wins in the end. I suggest you don't tape their mouth shut, but maybe your own.

- When your grandchildren are in your car and they are hurting or feeling sick, don't tell them "Just suck it up!" That may have worked in the dark ages, but you don't want them to grow up hating you.

Our Response: You don't have to immediately call "911," but seek to care and show, understanding. Be sensitive and supportive and only then take the appropriate action.

What I am seeking to emphasize is to use your heart and not always just your head. The Bible emphasizes that we ought to be a grandfather after God's own heart. If you don't know what that is, make an effort to look at the life of Christ. I will do it with you. He got it right every time.

Ask God to help you become like Christ in skin.

A Mind that Reveals

Grandchildren don't care how much you know
until they know how much you care.

Do you ask your grandchildren questions and wait for their response? Go ahead ask them what they are thinking. If you listen, it probably will reveal what is on their mind and in their heart. Don't settle for "fine." You may have to get them down on the floor in a wrestling match, take them on a ride, or visit McDonald's before their brain engages and their mouth runneth-over. An old proverb says:

Remember to engage your brain
before engaging your mouth;
so you don't have to disengage your foot from your mouth.

I have a grandson who is a thinker. He will give me the strangest looks. I have to deal with him differently than his brother. They are not just different ages they live at different levels. I can't treat them the same way. I have to think through my next move. One wants to play dominos, the other basketball. (By the way, I am great at both). ☺

Engaging your brain engages their heart.
Think it through to the heart.

Warning: Sometimes I am quick to give my children or my grandchildren a piece of my mind that I can ill afford to give? I have to give them a break and ask myself before I speak, "Am I being open- minded or close-minded?" A closed mind normally reveals a hard heart. Are we living in the present or are we dwelling in the past? God gave us two ears and one mouth which one do you guess we ought to use the most?

When the worst of our past lives in the present,
it steals the best from our future.

Words that Express

Your life can speak so loudly that
your grandchildren can't hear your words.

Let me remind you again that each of your grandchildren is different. So communicating with them comes in different forms and at different times. The best time to talk with them may not be the same. Get creative by observing, listening and then speaking. Remember that you might be thinking something that may not be worth saying. I wish I would have learned that sooner.

Warning: Your words should build up, not beat up!

I have one grandchild who opens up while driving in a car. We love to take her with us on trips. No video games allowed. I am able to speak into her life. Another loves to work with me. He gets a few dollars in his pocket, and I get to give him wisdom more valuable than gold. With another granddaughter I get down and play with her as she plays with dolls (including her favorite doll Madison), listen to her talk and express to her how much God and I love her.

Don't be stuck in a rut.
Figure it out.
Find out what works for each grandchild.

May I make a couple of suggestions? I will anyway. When you are talking to your grandchildren, and their mother or grandmother gives you the eye (you know the look), it might be best to change the subject. It will save you long conversations later. Trust me: Been there, done that!

Sometimes we need to say things just to see how they respond. It is amazing what comes out of their mouths and what we can learn. I was doing a project with my grandson and it got complicated, even for me, so I suggested we just wait until his dad got home. He looked at me with a confident look and said, "You can

do it Papa, it is going to be OK!" Guess what, I did it and it was OK!
Be honest even with your grandchildren.
You don't have to know everything.
It is worth the risk. You can do it!

Question: Have you earned the respect of your grandchildren? Do you expect your grandchildren to listen to your words although you have not earned their respect? Earning their respect starts with practicing what you preach.

Feet that Walk

Talk is cheap.
Walk your talk.

Back up your talk with your walk. Life is short enough. Love demands action. You say you love your grandchildren, show them, hug them, spend time with them, discover what they enjoy (this will change many times over the years) and take part. Share God's wisdom with them, avoid preaching. Let your life so shine before them that they see your good works and then they will want to follow your Father in heaven.

Two of our grandchildren live out of town. We attempt to make it a habit to call them with FaceTime or Skype. It is amazing how just spending a few minutes on line keeps the heart growing fonder. If you don't know how to use video communications, find someone to help you get set up. It's really not that hard. Find a teenager to help you.

You may not be able to live in the same community or state, but that is why God created highways and airports. So what is keeping you from grandfathering? Talk to your children and find out what works. Put a plan together. Your grandfathering will only be as good as your asserted effort.

Too often, life is what happens
when you are making other plans.

If you have the funds to go on vacations or weekend trips, make it a priority to plan time to visit with your grandchildren. Make it a funding priority.

My wife and I save up so we can be with our grandchildren who live out of state each year. We see it as an investment. How you invest in the lives of your grandchildren demonstrates what is really important to you.

Plan in one season and reap in another.
Excuses become a crutch for the uncommitted.
So stop making them.

Hands that Hold

They will know us by your love!
Your love can be shown in the palm of your hand.

You may not be one of those touchy-feely kinds of guys. Let me suggest loosening up. Meaningful and appropriate touch is good for both our grandchildren and our own souls. The first thing I do when I see my grandchildren is hug them, kiss them on the forehead, and tell them I love them and remind them that they are God's best. If they run and hide, I go hunt them down.

The most meaningful moment for me is when my youngest granddaughters grab my hand in the parking lot or crossing a street. They find security in the holding of a hand or the warmth of an appropriate and meaningful hug. Besides, you can remind them later when they are teenagers.

You may be the only Jesus
your grandchildren will ever hug.
Become the hands of God to reach out and to raise-up.

Here are some ways you can hold their hand and give them a hand up.

- Help them with their homework. You may not know anything about it, but you can cheer, not jeer, them on. "I don't know anything about it," is not an option.

- Go walk the dog with them. This is a great time for bonding.

- If they have their permit, let them drive your car. Teach them what you know. It won't take long. No! I am not nuts. (Just a little crazy… about my grandchildren.)

- If you have the resources, help your graduate with college. I am not saying you should pay all their way through. A care package works. Don't enable dependence, but serve to empower their independence through encouragement and support.

There are many ways you can give your grandchildren a hand that holds. Get creative. It starts with seeing, listening and caring.

A heart that cares becomes a hand that holds.

And a Life to be Transformed

When you allow God to transform you, He uses you to transform your grandchildren.

Scripture reads: *"Hear, O Grandfathers: The Lord our God, the Lord is one. Love the Lord your God with all your heart and with all your soul and with all your strength. These commandments that I give you today are to be on your hearts. Impress them on your children or grandchildren. Talk about them when you sit at home and when you walk along the road, when you lie down and when you get up. Tie them as symbols on your hands and bind them on your foreheads. Write them on the doorframes of your houses and on your gates."*
(Revised Grandfather Version – Deuteronomy 6:4-9)

I can't give my grandchildren what I have not first received myself. God wants to change us from the inside out. He wants His grace, mercy and love to leak out of us. God loved us so much that He sent His Son to die on a cross for us so that we could become the man, father, husband and grandfather He wants us to become.

When I understood that I was having a granddaughter without a dad in the home, I had to come to the realization that I had to change and be transformed. I could not give her what I had not received myself. So I changed!

The doing always comes out of the becoming,
not vice-versa.

Fall in love with your Savior, Jesus Christ first! Ask Him to change you from the inside out and allow Him to help you become a grandfather that is transformed and seeks to transform with eyes that see, a heart that feels, ears that hear, a mind that reveals, words that express, feet that walk and hands that hold. Only then can we have a life that can really "imagine the possibilities!"

Our Commitment

I will commit to intentionally ask questions, seek understanding and then listen without judgment to my grandchildren. I will seek to give appropriate and life giving advice and wisdom. I will not try to fix them but listen, support and only advise when appropriate and requested. I want to earn the right to transform by the life I choose to live and the legacy I choose to leave.

Reflections

Check the basics you struggle with most.

_____ eyes that see;
_____ ears that hear;
_____ a heart that feels;
_____ a mind that reveals;
_____ words that express;
_____ feet that walk;
_____ hands that hold;
_____ a life that transforms.

- Are you allowing God to transform you?

- Are you determined to help transform your grandchildren?

Prayer of Commitment

Dear Heavenly Father, I want to be a grandfather that is being transformed into the man you want me to become. Help me every day to commit my life to serving You by helping my grandchildren be transformed into the men and women you want them to become. It starts with me! Thank you for giving me a fresh start.
Amen!

Real-Life
From a loving Granddaughter

I have been blessed with four grandfathers; each one of them has positively impacted my life. By watching these men I have learned what love is. It is not just a word we say, but an action we choose every day. I have learned the importance of keeping your word, loyalty, how to have a strong work ethic, financial responsibility and the importance of family.

I have always had open communication with each of my grandfathers and feel like I can come to any of them with questions or concerns. Even though I lost one of them when I was a sophomore in high school he is still a huge influence in my life. The lessons I have learned from all of them will be with me the rest of my life. God has blessed me with two beautiful daughters of my own, who are not only blessed with their own grandfathers, but they have the pleasure of knowing three of mine as well. I hope and pray all the lessons I have learned from these wonderful men will be passed down in generations to come.

– Amber

Don't preach at or lecture your grandchildren.
Love them into who you want them to become.

Chapter 2
Invest Yourself Relationally

The "Be" Challenge

I have learned by experience that grandfathering is not just acknowledging you have grandchildren and spending more time with them. It is about making an intentional commitment and effort to help transform their hearts and lives. Action is required!

As a grandfather, you must make an intentional choice
to have a personal and open relationship with your grandchildren.
You must be there. Action required.

We have to invest our life relationally with our grandchildren and earn the right to speak into their lives. It demands us to invest in their lives on purpose.

Be Devoted

As a grandfather, you have a mandate. No more excuses. It will require your total devotion. You need to dedicate yourself to becoming a man who intentionally passes on a Godly legacy to your grandchildren, one that echoes now and for eternity. Your actions must speak louder than words, and your walk must follow your talk.

I decided when I became a grandfather that I would not put myself or my career first. Did I have to work? Yes! Did I have to make a living? Yes! But I also had to make a life. I would stop making excuses for why I could not or would not spend my time, talent or resources with or on my grandchildren. They would not grow up not knowing me, period!

Excuses become crutches for the uncommitted.

Be Honest with Yourself

Learn to be appropriately transparent.
Remember that God can change everything and everyone.

I will never be a perfect grandfather. My grandchildren have seen me at my best and my worst. I have had some honest talks with them about life – the good, the bad and the ugly. I have sought to be honest and transparent about my life, both successes and failures. I also have let them know that God forgives and changes everything.

We were celebrating a grandchild's birthday at a party not long ago. With two kids and seven grandchildren, there seems to be one every month. My son-in-law had to leave early and one of my grandsons was misbehaving. I was getting angrier by the minute.

Finally, my daughter was attempting to get the children in the car, but this grandson would not budge. I finally pick him up and slammed him into his car seat. He began to cry, but I felt great. I said to myself, "He needed discipline."

Although nothing was said, when I got home, I felt convicted that he was not the only one who was in the wrong. I was told all my life that two wrongs never make a right. I needed discipline.

When I saw him a couple of days later, I got down on my knees, looked into his eyes and asked him to forgive me. I don't really know if he even remembered what I had done, but he gave me a big hug and we became friends again.

I wish I could tell you that he or I have been perfect since, but I learned a great lesson and hopefully he did too. It is true that "Honesty is the best policy." It starts with us being honest with God first (He already knows it), with others and with ourselves.

*The inheritance you leave that really matters
is the one you live and give away.*

Be Intentional

*We need to intentionally invest in our grandchildren
with the purpose of helping them discover who they can become.*

My wife and I intentionally reach out to and celebrate all of our seven grandchildren. We have five in the Kansas City area and two in California. We make an intentional effort to see them when we can and make it a practice to communicate by any electronic means possible.

They must and will know us.
Love can be spelled i.n.t.e.n.t.i.o.n.a.l.

Even now I wish my own grandparents or parents had been more intentional. I am sorry to say my children seldom got a birthday or Christmas card. My parents did a lot of good things in their lives but my children did not have the opportunity to know them or experience that good. They were wonderful people and my children missed out. I did not want this to be part of my legacy.

What you want your grandchildren to say about you
is written with the pen of your life.

My wife and I go out of our way trying to make as many of our grandchildren's sporting events, ballet and musical performances as we can. They don't have to be the lead or the best. They just have to be there. If they are there, we want to make an intentional effort to be there also.

So what are you missing out on? Maybe you're saying "We don't live there. We live in Florida or Phoenix." There are too many absent grandparents and your grandchildren need you. I suggest you need to make an eternal decision? Move if it is possible! I know some of your grandchildren live in different states. If you can, live in one and travel often to the others by car, plane or the World Wide Web.

Once a year my brothers and sister made an intentional choice to plan a weekend with my mom and dad in Nevada. They were missionaries, so we all bunked in the church; slept on the floor, on the pews or in my dad's office. The strangest thing for my kids and my nieces and nephews was learning how to use an outhouse. The boys loved it that they did not get in trouble for not flushing. If they wanted to they could just go behind sagebrush and no one cared. My kids still remember those experiences.

We made an intentional choice
because family matters most.

We have carried on this tradition with our grandchildren. (Minus the outhouse and sagebrush). It doesn't have to be expensive just something they would not necessarily do without grandma or papa. If you can, involve the whole family that is even better. It is a great way for the family to stay in touch. They will be looking forward to this experience each year. If you can, intentionally plan these family gatherings way in advance. Make it fun, then tell them, "No excuses please."

Intentionality is a choice that can determine
how your grandchildren will remember your legacy.

P.S. If your family plans something and invites you, make an intentional effort to be there. Make sure they, your kids, pay and no excuses please. (Maybe not).

Your Commitment

I will dedicate myself to the "be" challenge. I am committed to building a personal and open relationship with my grandchildren. I will be there. I am committed to no more excuses. I will be honest with myself and be willing to make the appropriate changes in order to earn the right to speak by the way I live. And I will intentionally choose to invest in my children and grandchildren's lives. I want to write the legacy of my life by the way I live and by my being there.

Reflections

- What is keeping you from being the grandfather you need to become? What excuses are you continually using?

- Are you being honest with yourself about who you are as a person, father and grandfather? Are you willing to commit to changing?

- Are you intentionally investing in your children and grandchildren? Are you helping or hindering them?

- What would it take to change?

Prayer of Commitment

Dear heavenly Father you know the kind of man
I am and the kind of life I have been living. Please help
me make the intentional choices that will lead me to
become the father and grandfather you want me to be.
I want to be the kind of man that is
committed to leaving a legacy.
Amen!

Real-Life Grandfathering

As I have gotten farther into grandfathering, I can see much clearer what an influence we have on our grandchildren. One thing my wife and I did early in our grandchildren's lives was to participate in as many of their activities as we could. We are a sports-oriented family, so we would always try to attend their games and would always get hugs and a thank you for being there. To me, this was our way of keeping a closer relationship with them.

I also had the privilege to take each of our eight grandchildren on a canoe-camping to Canada's canoe country. What a blessing that was to be able to fish, cook and pray with them in the beautiful outdoors. On one of our trips, we were canoeing, and my grandson said, "Grandpa, how can anybody say there is no God when we see scenery like this?" This made my trip.

We recently received an email from one of our grandsons. His closing statement was, "Thanks, Grandma and Grandpa, for being the role models you have been." The little eyes are watching!

– Marvin

I have three kids and six grandchildren. One of my concerns is that so many grandparents abandon their responsibilities. They may get an RV and become snowbirds in Florida for a few months and forget about their grandchildren. Scripture teaches us that we are to pass on what we have learned to our grandchildren. For example, I employ my grandchildren to cut my yard and other manual labor activities. Each time they do it I have them pick up the tools and put them away. Anyone can cut grass but the important thing is to teach them life principles like a strong work ethic. These principles will last for their lifetime!

– Harold

Chapter 3
What Really Matters

If you want to leave a great inheritance, don't think it is necessarily about leaving them stuff (even though nothing is wrong with
that). It is more about leaving them a legacy that will last beyond
your lifetime. All the physical things you leave will decay, but the
character and memories you leave will last for your grandchildren's
lifetimes. What will stand out in their mind and hearts will be how
you communicated with your life the things that really matter for
now and for eternity?

You Love Them

Love is an intentional choice, not just a feeling. We have talked
about being intentional before. Repeating is good for the soul. I
wish I could get it the first time. Loving our grandchildren should
be pursued at all costs. It is not provisional but unconditional and
permanent.

Love is a choice we make every day.
So glad God does.

Love should not be viewed as a noun but as a verb. It is more caught than taught. Maybe you are asking what that means. When you say, "I love you," it must be lived out in action. Words are cheap. It can't be just words in a birthday or Christmas card. Putting your words into action will cost you some of your time, talent, treasure and touch.

My grandchildren's mom and dad
or grandmother can be a big help.
Humble yourself and ask for help in discovering
the love languages and interests of your grandchildren.

When you have seven grandchildren it can be very challenging because each one is so very different. I know many of you have many more. Because each child is unique, allow God to show you how to love them. Parents can give you some keen insights, but in many cases they are not around. It is becoming more and more normal that the family unit is fractured by divorce or an absent parent.

If you are dealing with grandchildren living in a difficult family situation you might want to get some family counseling or search for resources (i.e. library, website, other grandparents) that will educate you on how you can provide loving support. Seek with a loving heart to be part of the solution not add to the problem.

Aren't you glad God loved us where we are? (John 3:16) Christ can unconditionally love our grandchildren through us. Become him in skin.

Your actions should speak so loud that
your grandchildren can see and hear your love.

You Honor Them

Honor desires and believes the best in other children and grandchildren. They demand our dedication and devotion.

You honor your grandchildren by honoring
and respecting their parents, whenever possible.

Let me deal with a touchy subject. I know I went through this. You may be thinking in your mind that just because someone fathered your grandchildren that does not automatically earn them the right to be called or honored as their father. The bottom line is, it's really not what you or I think as a grandfather but what does your grandchild think and feel? If they see them as a parent, then you need to honor them when dealing with your grandchildren. To choose otherwise is to dishonor your grandchildren.

You may have grandchildren who were born without the advantage of marriage. The father or mother may not be in the picture. It is not your place to continually run them down, especially in front of the child. It might be best if you said nothing at all and ask God to change them. There may come a day when this child might want to meet their biological parent. It is up to you to show honor to the child by keeping your feelings to yourself and asking God to protect them.

There may be situations where you first have to love and honor your grandchildren and bring them under your protection because of abuse. This may be a very hard decision, but for the sake of your grandchildren it should be considered an option. Let me say it again. In this case they need someone like you who will cherish them no matter what.

Ultimately, you want them to accept the God-parent who will never leave them or forsake them.

You Serve Them

This may be our biggest challenge. I don't know about you but many find it easier to be served than to serve. Or when serving, you might be thinking, "What is in it for me?" Can we serve our grandchildren without expecting a specific return? Can we cherish and care for them with love being our only motivation. In many ways our relationship with our grandchildren has the same level of commitment as our marriage should have. It should not be one-sided but both-sided. What is best for them should also be best for us.

Serve them not out of social requirement but because of God's love in you. The only way they learn to serve is for you to teach and show them.

You will never stand as tall as a grandfather than when you stand from your knees.

In the book of John in the Bible, there was a debate among Christ's disciples about who would be the greatest when Christ overthrew the Roman Empire. They were defining leadership about a "what," holding a position (like grandfather) instead of about a "who," Chief Servant Leader" (CSL).

The disciples began to argue over who should have the right to sit next to Christ's throne in this newly formed Kingdom. Christ never said that he would be establishing an earthly kingdom at that time. What Christ was referring to was the cross that would become his throne on earth.

So in John 13:1-17 Christ gave them and us an illustrated sermon on who we are to become. He showed how we can become the "CSL" of our families. If you are going to truly leave a legacy that echoes into eternity, you have to become a servant of all. You are to descend into greatness. What Christ did that day illustrated to them and to us how we need to serve our wife, children and grandchildren. Oh, everyone!

You have to admit that as grandfathers we would rather do things with our grandchildren that we like to do, such as fishing, watching sports or shooting things. It is not high on our list to change diapers, help with homework or watch them with no apparent reward. Everything counts, so step up to serve and don't call it babysitting, call it grand-sitting. Someday they will be watching you.

I am not saying this will be easy. Many of us are too insecure to take the lower road. Washing feet will demand you set aside your personal position and power. It also may mean you get on the floor and roll around with your grandchildren, maybe even wearing a princess crown or playing "choo choo" with a toy train. It may mean you take your life in your hands and teach your teenager how to drive. It may mean going to your grandson's ballgame when your favorite pro team is playing on cable. It may mean going to your granddaughter's recital or ballet and pretending you love it. Remember, you do love it because you love them.

It is not our role to tell them they could do better or they are awful. Tell them they have potential and then take them to the batting cages or shoot baskets, (What no basketball hoop? Put one in your drive way) or fund some ballet lessons.

It is hard to get over ourselves;
only those who are really secure can go down to rise up.

You Support Them

You support them best by calling the best out of them.

Over the years, I would hug my children and grandchildren and tell them that they are God's best, but they have to be who they are. If they were misbehaving I would tell them that they were not being who they are.

Scripture tells us in Genesis 1 that when God created the earth he said "It was good." (vs. 25) But when he created Adam and later Eve in His own image God proclaimed indeed now all of creation was "very good." (Vs. 26-31)

The Message says it this way, "It was good, so very good!" One version reads, "So very good, excellent in every way." When you and your grandchildren were made in God's image you really were his best. God is not the problem here. God only makes the very best.

One evening I got a call from my oldest grandchild. I rarely got a call, so I immediately knew that something was up. She was about 13 at the time.

She said, "Papa is it really true that everyone is born the best?"

"Yes that is true," I replied. "According to the Bible everyone is made in the image of God and He only makes the best."

She hesitated and then asked, "Are you really sure?"

"Yes, I am really sure." "Why are you asking? Are you misbehaving?"

She quickly responded, "I have to go now!"

She had been disobeying and her parents reminded her that she was not being the best. She insisted that she was not the best. They encouraged her to call me. So she did. Your grandchildren need to realize that their behavior does not have to define or confine them, but God uses these to refine them. He uses these to refine them into the men and women they can and will become.

You cannot bring the best out of your grandchildren until you realize that you too are God's best. We also have to become who we are.

The opposite of love is not hatred. It is indifference.
So stop being indifferent and go make a difference. Why?
Because your grandchildren really are God's best and so are you.

Your Commitment

I will commit to make an intentional decision to love, cherish, serve and support my grandchildren, their parents and grandmother.
I will not allow myself or my grandchildren to show them dishonor

or disrespect even though they may not have earned them.

Reflections

- How are you intentionally showing your unconditional love to your grandchildren?

- How are you showing honor and respect to your grandchildren and their parents?

- How are you serving your family and especially your grandchildren?

- How are you supporting your family and grandchildren?

Prayer of Commitment

*Dear Heavenly Father, you know that I have struggled
with the things in this chapter in my own life.
I know that your love for me has never been conditional.
If it were I would be in deep trouble.
Give me a love that drives me to honor,
serve and respect my grandchildren, their parents and others.
Where I have failed, give me a fresh start. Show me where to
start and give me the courage to forgive myself.
Amen!*

Real-Life Grandfathering

While visiting our daughter, my wife and I were told we were going to be grandparents. We were overjoyed at the news! The name selected for a girl was Lydia Marie. Her middle name, Marie would extend into the fourth generation. We were all set for her birth but also anxious.

About four months into the pregnancy our daughter was told there was virtually no chance that this was a viable pregnancy, they wanted to do surgery, because this tissue now represented a health hazard to our daughter. Our daughter refused to agree to that procedure. We all spent a tearful weekend with our church family offering prayers on behalf of our grandchild.

On the following Monday, we were all relieved to hear that she was much improved and the heartbeat was strong. A couple of months later, during a sonogram, our daughter was told the fetus had no arm buds and it was possible the baby would have deformed arms or perhaps no arms at all. But our daughter was pleased that her child appeared to be healthy enough to withstand the pregnancy and, arms or not, this baby would be loved abundantly.

In February 2005 we had a new granddaughter. She had 10 toes and fingers and two healthy arms. She was to be the delight of her family. Because of her trials and prayer, her name was altered slightly. Our daughter believed, as we did, that she was with us because of the grace of God, and her name is Lydia Grace Marie. She has long curly red hair and sparkling brown eyes. She is a joy to us!

Lydia has learned so much in her 8 years, and I watch in awe as she takes in her surroundings. It reminds me of the lyrics to a Louis Armstrong song: "I hear babies cry, I watch them grow, they'll learn much more than I'll ever know, and I think to myself, what a wonderful world."

– Bob

Chapter 4
Keep the Three A's in Mind

There are three "A's" every one of our grandchildren need. These will help mold their hearts and help build a solid foundation for our legacy as grandfathers.

Attention

Attention is spelled T-I-M-E. Words are cheap but time costs.
It is paid with our time, talent, treasure and touch.

When I was a youngster my family used to visit my grandparents at their home in Southern California. When my grandfather retired he always wanted to live by the water and spend some of his retirement time doing his favorite hobby and that was fishing.

When we used to visit them by this beautiful lake I would look at him in his boat fishing. As I observed him from the dock I wished he would teach me how to catch a fish. There were occasions he would take us out in his boat but I never once fished or caught a fish. To this day I have not caught a fish. The big one got away.

Sometimes your grandchildren can be an inconvenience, get in the way and demand more time than you want to give.

May I suggest that you intentionally
(there's that word again) plan activities
that require your grandchildren to get in the way.

My wife has come up with a great plan at Christmas. Our grandchildren look forward to this game every year. We give them a small gift but then the real fun starts. She makes up a scavenger hunt that involves the whole family. The grandchildren are given clues to test their knowledge of the true meaning of Christmas. Clues allow them to earn their special Christmas gifts – Cash!

Hallelujah! Then they have the experience of buying just what they want. Another hallelujah! What a novel idea. It becomes memorable and a lot of fun.

This game always draws their attention.
Be creative it is memorable.

Affection

I emphasized this before, but I'm not sure I can say it enough. Affection and appropriate touch are vital in helping a child feel loved. If you don't believe me ask your wife or mine. We cannot or must not forget the power of meaningful and appropriate touch. There's real power in a HUG!

It is not enough to say you love your grandchildren.
It needs to be seen, expressed and felt.

When I think of affection I think of big giant hugs. I am a hugger. No handshakes allowed with my grandchildren. If they sneak in, I go looking for them. I want to make sure every one of them know I affectionately love them. Words are cheap. Actions speak louder than words.

Maybe you say, "I am not a hugger!" There, you said it again.
Let me give you a piece of advice: "Get over it!"
There, I said it again.

Believe it or not, the best affection you can give your grandchildren sometimes has nothing to do with hugs or words. It may require that you simply be there. My grandson had several baseball games where he kept striking out. He just needed me to walk by him on the way to the car. He wasn't ready for words or hugs, but my presence and eye contact let him know I loved him and supported him. Our grandchildren need to know we love them, even when life throws them curve balls.

Your grandchildren need to know you are not going to
abandon them. Your children need to know it also.

The Scriptures reads:

> *Let the children come to me. Don't stop them.*
> *For the Kingdom of Heaven belongs to those who*
> *are like these children.* (Matthew 19:14).

Affirmation

Words really matter.

The old rhyme that reads, "Sticks and stones may break my bones, but words will never hurt me" is a lie. Words can hurt much more than sticks or stones. They destroy the spirit.

The best way to show affirmation is to take time to look in their eyes, ask questions, be quiet and listen. Do these four things and eventually they will want to listen to you.

When you do speak, do not be a fixer or lecturer. Do a lot of "Hmm," "Great," I am sorry." Be supportive, and you will earn the right to speak.

Remember you are to be a "cheerleader." Keep cheering even when they strike out, fall down or fail. You are the one who comes alongside and says, "It is going to be OK!" "God is on your side, and so am I." "Don't give up; be strong; keep going." "You really are God's best, and don't you forget it. Remember you have to become who you are." "God will love you and that will never, never, never change, no matter what." Sounds like something God would say.

Maybe you wonder what you should do or say. Think about this. Just say to your grandchildren what you want someone to say to you when you are down, discouraged or in the middle of defeat.

It might be a great time to say, "Group Hug!" It might be all the affirmation they need.

You need to expect and call the best out of your grandchildren.
God will meet you at your level of expectancy.
Strive for a "Triple A" rating.

Your Commitment

I will commit to intentionally show affection, affirmation and atten-tion to my grandchildren. These will become the outward evidences of my inward love and support. I will choose to build them up by honoring and praising them every opportunity I can.

Reflections

- What in your life is robbing you of the time you need to spend with your grandchildren? What can you do about it? Do you want to?

- What is keeping you from showing affection? Does it relate to your past, pain or personal rejection?

- In what ways are you showing affirmation that is coming from your heart? What is keeping you from the ability to affirm your grandchildren?

Prayer of Commitment

Father, some of the things in this chapter are difficult for me. Please give me the courage and the grace to be the kind of grandfather who shows attention, affection and affirmation. In those areas I lack give me the insight and willingness to change. I really want to strive for that "Triple-A Rating."
Amen!

Real-Life Grandfathering

We have five surviving children, 14 grandchildren and 8 great grandchildren. Grandparenting is important in our family, and we make it a priority to get together as often as we can.

Although several of them live in other parts of the country, we personally visit them as often as we can and call them at least once a month. We regularly have lunch with those who live nearby. We talk with them about their interests, friends and values, how they are doing and what is happening in their lives.

Commitment is the key! We make our family a commitment and as their grandfather I will be behind them through the good and the bad times.

– Harry

Grandfathering is a touch of heaven for me. It gives me the opportunity to pour into the lives of my grandkids. My whole perspective is different now. My legacy isn't in a career path it is in this next generation. There isn't a more important or empowering role for me. I want, more than ever, to insure that my grandkids know "who they are" and "what they have" in their relationship with their Heavenly Father. As the patriarch, I believe I play a critical role in this happening.

– Greg

Behind every problem you see
in your grandchildren are unmet needs.
Don't work so hard to fix problems but to meet unmet needs.

Chapter 5
Becoming Part of the Solution

As a grandfather, you need to become part of the solution by helping your grandchildren establish priorities and set boundaries that help set them feel free and meet needs that really matter. Your future and theirs depends upon it!

Real solutions are more caught than taught.

Establish Priorities

Priorities are keys to unlocking a future that really makes a difference for them, their families and their legacies. Most of us never think in those terms, because we think that is the role of the parents. That is true in the broader sense, but you can help by the example you live. I think many of us are aware that some parents are not good role models. But we can be!

Let me suggest to you that the best way to show what really matters in life is by demonstrating to your grandchildren what really matters in your own life.

You must help your grandchildren put into practice in the present who they need to become in the future.

A good way to start is by writing out what your priorities are and at whom these efforts will be directed. They are my relationships with God, my wife and my family. You notice that they all relate to people. People matter most!

You will never see a U-Haul behind a hearse.
The stuff does not matter eternally.
The people do.

I think many of us would write down the same thing. But there are questions we should ask of ourselves. "How am I doing?" Are God and my family my true priorities? In my daily living, do I nurture my relationships with God and family members through the way I spend my time, talent, treasure and touch. May I suggest that you do a close evaluation of your own life. Ask your family how you're doing. Do they feel less important than others things in your life, such as sports, hobbies, personal successes. (or you fill in the blank): _____

What matters most to you?
Do you spend your life succeeding at what really matters?

Help Set Boundaries

Are you part of the problem or becoming part of the solution?

Physical boundaries keep things in and keep things out. They do the same with people. What or who are you allowing in and keeping out? Are your grandchildren in or out? What are you allowing in that should not be there? What needs to be in and what needs to be out?

Maybe you are struggling with inappropriate language. If it is not appropriate in front of your grandchildren, it probably should not be said anywhere. Maybe there is some behavior that you would never do in front of them. Why is it appropriate anywhere?

Don't go from preaching to meddling.

Am I acting out in my life in ways I would never want my grandchildren to behave? Set boundaries in your own life that are realistic and appropriate for your grandchildren, regardless if they see them in their own parents.

Do as I say or just as I do?

Do a sincere inventory. Are you living your life in a way that illustrates to your grandchildren what is permissible, good or the best? Your priorities and boundaries become a living illustration that answers these questions for your grandchildren.

Yes, I am asking you to evaluate your whole life.

Meet Needs

Nothing is impossible with God.
Ask him first.

When I say a grandfather should help meet the needs of his grandchildren, I am not saying to give them all they want. If our grandchildren seek to have their needs met by the standards of the world, they will find themselves empty and always seeking more. Meeting a grandchild's desires can even hurt them. Focusing on fulfilling their desires may enable them rather than able them. We live in a country of enablers, people who are dependent on others and who believe they are entitled to that dependency.

With wisdom we can actively participate in a plan to meet the true needs of our grandchildren, and those needs will vary depending on their home environment. If your daughter or son is raising children as a single parent they may need help providing basic needs and even opportunities for enrichment, such as participation in extracurricular activities.

Each situation is different, so seek God's guidance on how you can serve your children and grandchildren well, be it financially, spiritually or as a loving mentor.

The ultimate road to happiness will be found when our grandchildren find true fulfillment, living a life that makes a difference now and for eternity. I have coached many a grandfather who has spent his life making a living but not a life, and not one that really mattered. Grandchildren matter!

"Happy is the man who finds wisdom,
and the man who gains understanding."
(Proverbs 3:13)

Some of the best things we can give to our grandchildren have nothing to do with things. Needs are best met by pointing them to what and who really matters. The things that will actually fill their emptiness! The question is have you discovered them for yourself?

You can't lead them to the place you have never been.

I talked to many grandfathers who don't have money or things, but they have much more. They produced the fruit that lasts a lifetime. My dad knew this.

Scripture says that we are to be like a tree that bears the fruit of the Spirit, which is love, joy, peace, longsuffering, kindness, goodness, faithfulness, gentleness and self-control. How are you doing? You notice that it is called the fruit of the Spirit, singular. The Spirit of God contains all of these. The best way we can meet our needs and those of our grandchildren is by sharing the fruit of this tree.

I want my grandchildren to know me by my love, joy, peace, etc.
They are my fruit inspectors.

Your Commitment

I will intentionally commit to setting the priorities and boundaries that will meet needs and help my grandchildren become

God's very best. I will focus my attention on the things in life that really matter and encourage my grandchildren to do the same. I will seek to be part of the solution, not the problem. I will allow God to produce His fruit in me and then allow it to leak out. I want my grandchildren to know me by my love, joy, peace, longsuffering, kindness, goodness, faithfulness, gentleness and self-control.

Reflections

- What priorities do I need to live out as a grandfather? List them.

- What boundaries do I need to set as a grandfather? List them.

- What are the needs that God is asking me to meet as a grandfather? List them.

- Which fruits of the Spirit are lacking in my life? List them. Now ask God for them!

Prayer of Commitment

My Heavenly Father, I so much want to serve my grandchildren by helping you help them establish biblical priorities and boundaries that will meet their unmet needs. Start you work in me! I know I can't lead them where I have never been myself. Do your work in

me and produce the fruit of your Spirit in me.
I ask that much fruit will be evident in my life.
Do whatever you need to do make that happen.
Amen!

Real-Life
From a loving Granddaughter

The ways my grandfather has impacted my life are endless. I was born in California, half a country away from my Oklahoma-based grandfather, so the visits from my grandparents were few. However, whenever they would make the trip out to California or when my family would fly out to meet them at their Colorado home, it was a huge event. We would go fly-fishing or skiing, and just operate as a full family unit. These childhood memories are some of the most vivid ones I possess.

My grandfather and I were not extremely close until my mother, brother and I moved to Oklahoma. After my parents got divorced, my family was in a state of uncertainty. My mother especially had a difficult time getting used to life as a single mother, so my grandfather had to step in and become an influential male presence in my brother and my lives. He also supported my family financially through the transitional period between my mother being a stay-at-home mom to having to find a full-time job while still nurturing her two young children.

One of the most thoughtful things that my grandfather did for me was to establish a Money Trust for my college education. If he and my grandmother had not looked ahead to my future, then I would be swamped with education loans and be fearful about how I was going to pay for my continuing education.

The emotional and financial stability that my grandfather offered me has gotten me to who I am today: a happy, loved, University of Tulsa student. Throughout the last seven years of my life, I have established a deep influential connection with my grandfather that has helped provide the basis for me to lead a successful life.

– Mikayla

Chapter 6
Build Memories,
not Just Moments

I love taking my grandchildren to Disney, to the playground or to the beach. These activities are fun but do they create memories that keep on keeping on even after this lifetime has passed. I don't want to sound like a scrooge because I do believe that having fun is very important. I am the first one to get on a ride at the park as long as it is not the roller coaster (scared of heights). While these create very important moments, I just believe we need to be committed as grandfathers to also create memories that stay with our grandchildren after we are gone. We really can build memories for a lifetime.

A lifetime runs out,
but eternity is a very, very long time!

Build...

Buildings that have no foundation will never stand the winds of time. Wow, how profound. Life's trials will come and go, but the foundations you help build in your grandchildren's lives will last for a life time.

Maybe you agree with me that our grandchildren grow up too fast. They seem to go from diapers to grade school through high school in a moment. What is built in them in these years will last the rest of their lives. Where do you fit in the building process, if anywhere?

The key words I think of when building anything is "structure" and "intentional." What kinds of structures are you intentionally building into your grandchildren's lives that are done with a purpose and done on purpose?

Build with purpose.
Build on purpose.

It's hard for your grandchildren to see God's purpose working out in their lives just as it is for us. God does not do anything by accident. All we have gone through is all part of what God wants to build in us. Year by year, challenge by challenge, decision by decision, God uses them all to build his image in us.

Think about how you can intentionally build in each of your grandchildren. Here are some things I want to build in my grandchildren and in myself.

It is more caught than taught.

- A hunger for the Word and a daily quiet time with God. Let them see you. Ask them how you might pray for them.
- A desire to serve God with their lives. Take them on some kind of mission trip near or abroad.
- Having a heart for the poor and have them participate with you gathering items that can be taken to the homeless shelter and have them go with you.
- Be an active member in their church. Sit and talk with them about what they are learning from their church involvement.

The world around us is in direct conflict with what we want to see in our grandchildren's lives. The world creates expectations that may have nothing to do with God's purposes. We must live and actively proclaim the truth over the lies. As a grandfather, I want to be one of the louder voices saying to our grandchildren that God loves them and has a wonderful plan for their lives. Words, thoughts and actions can build up or tear down, which do they hear and see from us?

What you want your grandchildren to remember
must be said and lived now.

Memories...

The best legacies you will ever leave
are the memories you create.

How do you want your grandchildren to remember you? It is a

life-sized question!

If I were to ask each of my grandchildren what was their most memorable moment I hope there are seven, one for each of my grandchildren. Why? Let me say it again, because they are all individuals. We must see them as individuals and seek to build memories that last for their life-times.

Memories are made over time.

I am sure all of my grandchildren will remember the great time we had at the lake, at an amusement park or on a Disney cruise. But what memories would each of my grandchildren recall as being special; working together on a project, a mission trip to the Navajo Nation, maybe playing Scrabble or Dominoes and beating Papa over and over again? Those memories have very specific meaning, because of the time and conversation we have while doing them.

As I look back on my own days as a grandchild, I have few memories. I am not judging my grandparents, because I never really knew them. Their lack of grandparenting is no excuse for me.

I want to change history and memories on purpose.
Memories by accident can be scary.

Build, structure, and create the times you want to live and the memories you want to leave. Recently we spent a week in Breckenridge, Colo., and the best things I did with our grandchildren was make snow angels. It did not cost us one dime. It was not the reason for the trip (Thanksgiving); it was simply spontaneous and great fun. We have the pictures!

Your grandchildren will not judge you by the car you drive,
the house you live in or by the stuff you own
but by the memories you live and leave.

For a Lifetime

Maybe you're thinking, "Wow, for a lifetime!" "There is plenty of time for that." Really? Only God knows for sure, and you ain't God! So what are you waiting for?

How much lifetime do we really have left?
Oh, you don't know!
You might want to get on with it now.

May I make a suggestion? Well, I'm going to do it anyway. Ask each of your grandchildren this simple but leading question, "If I could do anything for you or with you that I can afford, what would you like most?" What would they say? If you don't know, at least ask. I promise I will, too!

Remember...
Money and stuff will be spent and rust away
but memories last for a lifetime.

When you ask them what you could do for them remember they are different ages. You may need to ask the parents for some insights. My list is by ages. Here we go...

Gabby (19 yrs) – Call me on the phone and ask me how my day is going. (She is in college) Send me a care package of things you know I like. (A little cash won't hurt.)

Kayla (14 yrs) – Have serious and meaningful conversations with me. Take me on mission trips with you. (Love too.)

Alex (11 yrs) – Support me at my sporting events (quietly). Tell me about the Bible. Share what you do by taking us to events like Iron Sharpens Iron men's conferences when you speak. (Kissing up, it's working.)

Dylan (8 yrs) – Take me to the park. Play dominoes with me (Double 15's) (You can hear the parents saying, "Thank you! Thank you!")

Bella (7 yrs) – She was wishing it was Christmas so her grandmother and I could take her to the snow. (When we went to Colorado last year, we had a great time making snow angels.)

Hallie (6 yrs) – Take her to get donuts on those mornings we have her overnight. (The other kids are invited.) Tell her stories about when I was a little boy. (I hope I can remember. That was a long time ago.)

Danny (5 yrs) – He loves it when I take him out to eat. He also wants me to help him learn how to play tennis. (I think tennis lessons are on the horizon. His dad and his other grandpa are very good tennis players.)

Reminder: YOUR greatest investments or achievements are not found
in your "what's" - possessions, power, privilege or prestige -
but in your "Who's" - God, your wife, family and
the legacy you live and leave.

Your Commitment

I will intentionally commit to building relational
and godly memories in the lives of my grandchildren.
I will commit to spending my life now in a way
that leaves eternal dividends and rewards.

Reflections

- How is the building going? What do you see in your grand-children, and what do you need to do?

- What memories are you seeking to leave on purpose? How are you being intentional?

- What memories would you like to build in your lifetime? Go for it!

Prayer of Commitment

Dear Heavenly Father, thank you for the life I have left to build
memories in the lives of my family and grandchildren.
Show me who I need to be and what I need to do. Allow me to live
and leave a legacy that I will be proud of and that
my grandchildren will be pleased to talk about after I am gone.
I want them to know first that I loved and followed you
with all of my heart, mind, soul and strength,
Amen!

Real-Life
From a loving Grandson

Grandpa takes me to the movies and dinner when a good action film is at the theater. WE drove together to Colorado to go skiing last winter.

He takes me to the Friday night Fish Fry during Lent. I always get a double order of shrimp only. I love shrimp.

He gives me advice on my merit badges toward my Eagle Scout rank. He and grandma are advising me to join the Air Force after college. I may join the Air Force ROTC in High School next year. I am in eighth grade now.

We work together on the yard work at his house.

– Nicholas

CHAPTER 7
Name them by Name

As a grandfather, you need to daily pray for and, when possible, pray with your grandchildren individually and name them by name. You need to plant seeds of God's love, courage and hope in their lives and in their spirit.

Through Prayer

Praying for your grandchildren is the next best thing to being there!

My wife and I have made it a practice over the years to pray every day for each of our grandchildren, specifically and by name. Some of you are thinking that you can't or don't pray out loud. Of course you don't have to, but practice does make perfect.

For me praying is like talking to my best friend or my own Heavenly Father. I don't pray in my King James nobody-can-understand voice. For example:

> *"Oh, holy God of the universe, your humble*
> *worthless servant comes to you*
> *with fear and trembling asking you*
> *to consider my unworthy prayer."*

I don't know about you, but I think if I prayed that way God would just crack up. I know some people pray that way and God loves a good laugh, but that is not how we need to talk to our Heavenly Dad about His grandchildren. Yes, they were His before they were ours. He knew them before the foundation of the world. He knows them better than we will ever know them.

He has already seen our grandchildren's tomorrows.

We should pray as a loving grandfather to a loving, all-knowing, all-caring, all- powerful Father. When you do pray, be as specific as possible! That is not for God but for you. It keeps you seeking and listening to your grandchildren. God knows exactly what you and your grandchildren need, but it keeps you in tune with the needs and wants of your grandchildren. God loves to answer needs and wants.

What is cool is that God loves to use me to represent Him in skin.
Thanks God!

Through Praise

If you plant seeds of fear and despair
in your grandchildren, you will reap victims.
If you plant seeds of faith and hope, you will reap victors.

What do you see in your grandchild that is praiseworthy? Think on those things. Call those praiseworthy attributes out of them. Most of the time, they will not see it. They will have a tendency to see themselves in light of others or superstar heroes.

When your grandchildren are down, praise them up.

Maybe you are thinking, "You don't know my grandchildren." I don't need to know them. Scripture says I ought to think on whatever is true, noble, just, pure, lovely, of good repute and praiseworthy (Philippians 4:8). These are the very attributes I ought to think of and call out of my grandchildren. These are what God is calling out of us.

Their circumstances, past or pain do not have to define them.
God wants to use our grandchildren and refine them.

Every week, I try to text my children and grandchildren (who have phones) and tell them I am praying for them, that I love them and miss them. They always text me back, "Thank you grandpa."
You might say, "I don't text." May I suggest you learn how to text for them. They will appreciate it. Start getting in the real world.
P.S. Wives like it, too.

May I suggest you remember Paul's writings; I try to! *"Finally brethren and grandfathers (my words), whatever things that are true, whatever things that are noble, whatever things that are just, whatever things that are pure, whatever things that are lovely, whatever things that are of good report, if there is any virtue and if there is anything praiseworthy -- meditate on these things."* (Philippians 4:8)

Don't simply mediate on these things but tell your grandchildren how much these mean to you when you see them in their lives. They also may notice them in your life. Wouldn't that be really cool? Then you can say like Paul, *"Grandchildren, the things which you learned and received and heard and saw in me, (Papa Dan) these do, and the God of peace will be with you."* (Philippians 4:9)

Through Encouragement

Courage is the result of encouragement.
Don't discourage, encourage.

Encourage means to bring courage. Our grandchildren get plenty of discouragement from all kinds of people, places and things. Our role is to encourage them. It seeks to build up, not tear down. It seeks to move them forward, not keep them in neutral. Encourage them to move toward God's will and His purpose for their lives. They need to know you love them and are there for them. It will make all the difference in the world if not to them, it will for you.

To encourage is another form of building up. (Chapter 6) You notice I did not say "brag up." When you only "brag up," you are building up their ego but not necessarily their hearts. I have seen too many parents or grandparents brag on their child, which only makes them full of pride. Scripture declares that "Pride goes before a fall and a haughty spirit before defeat." (Proverbs 16:18) Some of the most insecure people I have ever met are also some of the most prideful. Are you an encourager or a bragger? Trust me, they are not the same.

Humility takes courage.

Do you know that correction also can be a form of encouragement? I have said plenty of times to my children and grandchildren that their behavior does not reflect who they really are or who they can become. (Not those exact words.) At the time I provide this encouragement, there are times that I can see on their faces that they strongly disagree with me. This will likely happen to you too. Stay strong but gentle at the same time. Stay in control and remember your words must build up your child and grandchild.

Correction is in order.
We have to help them want to want God's best.

Physical correction is not our job as a grandparent, unless the children are our fulltime responsibility. That is the role of the parent. My role is to help them with their stinking thinking. With encouragement in mind, I need to help them when what they are thinking or saying is just not true. When the enemy is telling them a lie, God, through me, can give them truth.

Stinking thinking leads to stinking living.
Encouragement sets us free.
Yes, even through tears

It takes a secure grandfather to express his heart through his tears.

I don't know about you, but I don't cry. My eyes leak! Some might argue grandfathers don't cry. Let me say it again; "Get over it!" Tears are a sign that you have a heart. True tears come from the soul.

When my oldest granddaughter graduated from high school, I cried. When each of my grandchildren was born, I cried. When I heard that a grandchild received Christ, I cried. When they are happy or succeed I am a weeping grandfather. I am proud of it!

Tears that come from the heart keep the heart tender. If you say you are not a crier, may I suggest you pray for tears! Scripture says, "Jesus wept." If you don't believe me, look it up! (John 11:35) He wept at the death of a friend and the sorrow it brought to the family. I think he weeps for the sorrow death brings to humanity especially when it is spiritual death! If you understand the heart of the Father and His love for you and your grandchildren, you will be pleased to shed tears.

Your grandchildren are all unique to God. Love, pray, encourage, and when possible, weep for them as God does. What God says about His Son He says about me and my grandchildren. He says to Gabby, Kayla, Alex, Dylan, Bella, Hallie and Danny, "You are my children whom I love and in whom I am well pleased."

If you don't know what to do - pray;
If you don't know what to say - praise;
If you don't know what to think - encourage;
If you don't know what to feel - weep.
That is what Jesus did.

Your Commitment

I will intentionally commit to becoming a man of prayer.
I will pray for my grandchildren every day, and when possible,
in their presence or by any other means.
I will name them by name and seek God's will,
presence and plan in their lives.
Whenever I can, I will pray, praise, encourage and,
yes, weep for them. I will ask God to protect them
from the enemy who seeks to kill, steal and destroy.

Reflections

- What is keeping me from praying for each of my grandchildren each day? List it.

- What do I see as praiseworthy in each of my grandchildren? List them.

- Where do my grandchildren need encouragement? List them.

- What is keeping me from weeping? What is holding me back? List it.

Prayer of Commitment

*My Heavenly Father, thank you for the opportunity
to minister in the lives of my grandchildren. I promise to
pray for them on a daily basis. Show me how to pray.
Teach me how to praise and encourage. Let my heart break
over the things and people that break your heart. Mold me and
make me into the man and grandfather you want me to become.
Amen!*

Real-Life Grandfathering

My wife, Joyce and I have been blessed by five wonderful grandchildren. I can honestly say that when our first grandchild was born, I was excited as much as when our first child was born. I remember seeing a great bumper sticker that said, "If I knew that grandchildren would be this good I would have had them first."

Being with your grandchildren is always a thrill and I miss them greatly when I can't be with them. The relationship with them is a unique opportunity that I am very thankful for. When I spend time with them I am able to show my sincere interest in them and what they are doing. I am able to demonstrate to them the priorities in my life beginning with my relationship with God through Jesus Christ.

As a grandfather I trust that I will live my life in such a way as to model important things such as working hard, helping others and showing unconditional love for those who come into my life.

Even when I can't be with my grandchildren I am able to pray for them. I pray that God would protect them from physical, emotional and spiritual harm. I also thank God daily for what He is going to do in their lives.

My life motto is, "When life comes to an end there is only three things that will count – the people I loved, the people who loved me and what I did in the service for God," nothing else is really going to count for much. My grandchildren are among those whom I love most in my life and I value their love more than I can say.

– Craig

Tell your grandchildren they are God's best.
But they have to become who they are.

SECTION 2:

Leaving a Legacy
for
Your Grandchildren

Chapter 8
Your Work is Never Done

As grandfathers, realize that as long as you are alive your ministry to your grandchildren is never done. So you need to continually...

Expand Yourself

As a grandfather, when you get stuck in neutral
you end up making a lot of noise
while going nowhere.

As a young man learning to drive, my dad gave me my first lesson. When I attempted to back the car out of the driveway I accidently shifted it into neutral. I started revving the engine, but the car would not move. After some time revving the engine I finally told my dad that the car wasn't working. He smiled and patiently told me, "No car will work until you take it out of neutral."

Many, if not most, grandfathers will spend their living in neutral, waiting for something to happen. Like the car stuck in neutral we end up making a lot of noise but going nowhere. What gear are you stuck in?

You will only be able to give away
what you have first discovered for yourself.

Are you stuck going nowhere or are you moving toward God's will and purpose in your life? Your personal and spiritual growth becomes part of God's will, purpose and legacy for you to live and to leave. Will your children and grandchildren want to follow your example? What are you showing them? Where are you leading them?

Don't miss out.
God is not through with you.

Give Yourself Away

One of the greatest paradoxes in life
is that when you are willing to give it all away,
you really gain it all.

What or who are you holding onto? Maybe you are hanging onto yourself for dear life. What has God given to you that He is now asking for you to give? Look and see. It probably is something to do with your time, talent, treasure and touch. Have I left something out? Oh, He wants that too!

When I was in my early 50s, God said to me that He wanted me to resign my job as one of the pastors of a wonderful church. Churches don't pay that well, but they do pay every two weeks. I honestly told God, "Wait, another day. See me in a few years. Talk to me when I have enough money in the bank, more time, etc." The problem was not with God; it was with me. I would not be the man or the grandfather I am now if I was not willing to give it all and let go.

God has heard all the good excuses.
It is only when we let go we can then let God.

God loved me enough to lay me up in a hospital bed to tell me that He had a "Greater Yes! - a greater potential and destiny for my life." My wife drove three hours to find me ready to go into surgery. I told her I had to resign the church and do what God was calling me to do. She said, "It is about time!" That began the rest and the best of my life. A few months later, my first book, "Finding Your Greater Yes" was published. Your "Yes" and God's "Yes" equals a "Greater Yes." God has a greater yes, a greater potential and destiny, for you also.

Trust me; your "Greater Yes" must include your grandchildren.

What excuses are you making right now that are keeping you from becoming the man and grandfather God wants you to become? What are you hanging onto that is keeping you from your potential and destiny, which in turn is robbing you of your God-given potential and legacy?

Your children and grandchildren are watching your choices.
How are you allowing God to change you?

Reproduce Yourself

God has already prepared in you
what he wants to conceive in you
and birth out of you.

The great artist Michelangelo stood staring at a huge piece of marble for months before he began his artistic endeavor. What was he doing?

During those months of staring, many asked what he was doing. He simply said, "I am working." He was mentally formulating the image that would emerge from the giant stone. He saw its' potential. He saw this stone for what it could become in the hands of a skillful artist. When he was finished creating in his mind what it could become, he began to chip away what did not belong.

Just as Michelangelo chipped away at his "David," God is even more skillfully chipping away to display what he wants to see in our lives and in the lives of our grandchildren. He is removing what does not belong and He is revealing his and our best.

Trust God, He knows what He is doing.
He wants to chip away what does not belong.

Although you may know that God is at work in our lives to change our character, this process takes time. We must decide on a daily basis whether we will follow Him willingly. Are you willing to open your life to the influence of the master artist? He wants to create a masterpiece from your life, but you must be willing.

Reminder: What God has dreamed for you as a grandfather
can echo now and for eternity
through the legacy you live and leave.

Your Commitment

I will intentionally commit to becoming a grandfather who
continues to grow and who will choose to pass on a
Godly legacy to my family and grandchildren.

Reflections

- Are you going nowhere or are you moving toward God's will and purpose in your life?

- What or who is keeping you from expanding your relationship with your grandchildren?

- What excuses are you making right now that are keeping you from becoming the man and grandfather God wants you to become?

- What are you hanging onto that is keeping you from your potential and destiny that in turn is robbing you of your legacy?

- Are you willing to open your life to the influence of the master artist? What is keeping you from doing that?

Prayer of Commitment

Heavenly Father, make me into the man and
grandfather that carries your presence with me.
Give me the courage to give myself freely to you and to others.
Nothing I have is mine, it is all yours. Do as you will!
Make me into a man that others would emulate, a man
who reflects your love, grace, forgiveness and generosity.
I can't do this on my own so please go before me and guide my path.
Amen!

Real-Life
From a loving Granddaughter

I have a big family; we are close and love being together. I fully attribute this rare family characteristic to my grandfather.

Throughout the years I have seen him sacrifice for his family. He has given up his valuable time when any of us have needed him. I have seen him give up money to take his grandchildren back-to-school shopping or buy them tires because they needed them. I've also seen him give up money to take the whole family on vacation....multiple times. He has given up rooms in his house, cars in his garage, and food off his table to make sure his family is not only taken care of, but happy! Now, as we all get older, he is trying to share his faith with his children and grandchildren. When he does this he is showing that he is willing to sacrifice the close family that he has worked so long for, so that their eternity is saved.

Many grandfathers teach their grandchildren how to play baseball or chess. They might teach how to negotiate a deal or how to stay true to their word. My grandpa has taught me the only way to keep our family together eternally is to make sure they all know the Lord.

– Heather

Put in practice in the present with your grandchildren what you want to see in them in the future.

Chapter 9
Know Who You Are

You cannot give your grandchildren what you do not have.
You have to know first who you are

What do you need to know to find your God-given identity, significance, purpose and potential for you and your grandchildren? It does not just happen. It has to be called and lived out!

John 10:10 proclaims to every one of us (and our grandchildren) that *"The thief (Satan) comes only to kill, steal and destroy but I have come that they (you) may have life and have it to the full."* *(NIV)*

As a grandfather, you can have the privilege of helping your grandchildren answer the questions of life that will determine their future and potential. Before you can do that, however, you have to know and answer these questions for yourselves.

Ephesians 2:10 reads, *"For we (you) are God's workmanship, created in Christ Jesus to do good works, which God prepared in ad-*

vance for us (you) to do." (NIV)

The Message paraphrases it this way, *"God does both the making and the saving. He creates each of us by Christ Jesus to join him in the work he does, the good work he has gotten ready for us to do, work we had better be doing."*

*Grandchildren are part of the good work God has called us to do!
You can't see God do a good work in them through you
until you allow God to do this good work in you.*

Answer these four questions to better understand who you are. As you better understand who God made you to be, you will be better equipped to help your grandchildren discover who God made them to be.

Who am I?

"You are his workmanship…"

*God is working in you what he wants to work out and through you!
God never says, "Oops."*

This question addresses your identity. Who you are-your identity-is unique to how God created you as an individual. You are God's very best! You are special to him and there is no one like you. You were created in the image of God, and He makes only the very best. The average grandfather doesn't know who he is. The answer is not found in where you come from, what you do or what you own. Your identity is not defined or determined by what your career says, what others say, what the world says, what your bank accounts say or what your past says. It is about what God says. He says you are his workmanship, created in his image, and he makes only the very best. No other creation can boast of that truth.

When my twin brother and I were born, we were classified as deaf. They could not determine any physical reason why we could not hear, which led later to the inability to speak. Many considered us "deaf and dumb." This led to many challenges in school.

Other than these inabilities, we were very healthy. Still, kids made fun of us and called us stupid. Fortunately at the time, we could see them making fun of us but we could not hear them. It created a lot of problems in school, which led to anger on my part. I finally begin to lash out, which got me into a lot of trouble. I knew I was not stupid! God knew it, too!

When I was 9, my parents sold everything and we moved to Nevada to serve as missionaries among the Native Americans. I did not understand what they were doing. I did not know at the time that it would change our lives forever.

In preparation for the move my parents had each of us examined by doctors who arranged tonsillectomies for my twin and me. When we came out of surgery, something incredible happened. We could hear! I believe God honored my parents' decision to serve as missionaries and gave us our hearing. My brother and I would become an extension of God's grace through ministry, speaking, writing and coaching throughout the world.

*You will never see your grandchildren as they really are
until you see yourself as God sees you,*

as his workmanship, his masterpiece, as his very best.

Whose am I?

*"You are his workmanship **created in Christ Jesus…**"*

In Christ you can do all things,
apart from him you can do nothing
that will leave a legacy now and for eternity.

This question addresses your significance, value and worth. In Christ you can do all things but apart from Christ you can do nothing that echoes now and for eternity. What you see and do with your grandchildren can have eternal ramifications. Do you find your significance, value and worth in the things you own, your "what's?" Or do you find your value in your "who's," first with Jesus Christ and your family.

The average grandfather doesn't know whose they are. They can't give their grandchildren what they have never received for themselves. As my grandchildren grow, I watch the steps they attempt, enjoy the sounds they make and delight in every aspect of their growth. I am a proud "Papa." I believe God our Heavenly Father sits on the edge of his great throne and looks down at every one of his children, expressing joy, excitement, gladness, and yes, sometimes sadness. You see if God ever stopped loving you, He would have to stop loving Himself. God can stay pleased with you because he sees you through the eyes of his heart and he sees you as you could become.

He sees who you can become in Christ Jesus.

One of my granddaughters was riding in the back seat, buckled into her car seat when she said to me, "Papa, Papa, I love you!" At that moment she could have asked for practically anything she wanted. I quickly asked her, "How much do you love me?" She spread her arms as wide as she could and said, "This much Papa, this much."

As I sat there beaming, I could hear a still small voice say to me, "That is how much I love you too, but when I spread my arms they engulf the entire universe." I noticed her arms and body were making a cross, and I wept.

It is amazing what grandchildren can teach us about ourselves ... our significance, value and worth. God can teach you through your grandchild that your condition or circumstances do not have to define or confine you or them but God can use circumstances to refine and re-find you. He uses them to propel you to your legacy.

Why was I Created?

"You are his workmanship created in Christ Jesus
for a good work..."

God created us for a good work
that we must do.

This question addresses your purpose, which is why God created you in the first place. When it comes to your grandchildren, you must help them find their good work for their lives… but you have to find yours first.

You can't give what you do not possess.
Or lead where you have never been.

The question you need to answer is, "Why was I created? It is not to live 70 years or so and then just die. Your purpose flows from answering the first two questions: who and whose I am?

You were created for a good work. Part of that good work is being the grandfather God intended you to be. Instead of living a life emboldened by God's purpose, most people live hemmed in by their own insecurities driven by a false identity and tasks that lack eternal significance. Your purpose should be driven by what God says, not by your condition or your circumstances.

I choose to live where I live not to please myself, but driven by the passion and love I have for my grandchildren. I am a better man because I made a choice to serve God and my family first. I will not necessarily be remembered by my speaking, coaching or writing but by the Godly legacy I leave. That is my true purpose!

May your grandchildren imitate the God in you!
He is more caught than taught.

What am I Destined to Become?

"You are God's workmanship created in Christ Jesus to do good works which God prepared in advance for us to do." - Ephesians 2:10

Before you were created,
God saw who you could become.

This question addresses your potential, your destiny and your legacy. You need to know that God loves you. He is not pleased with you because you are so good, go to church every Sunday or can quote many scriptures. He is pleased with you because he already sees who you can become. You are part of a great story and your children and your grandchildren are key players.

My wife and I took one of our granddaughters on a trip to an Indian reservation in Arizona. We did Vacation Bible School for a week in two different sites. Our granddaughter saw real poverty and despair for the first time in her young life. As she spent the week serving, loving and caring for these precious children, she said to us on the way home, "All my life I wanted to be an actress. I have changed my mind. I want to be a missionary-actress." Our purpose became a good work, and she is becoming part of our legacy.

Grandfathering is attempting to see grandchildren
both in their current reality and also in their future potential.

Before you or your grandchildren were ever thought of by fellow human beings, God had a purpose, plan and future. I am reminded again of God's declaration, *"I know what I am doing, I have it all planned out, plans to take care of you, not abandon you, plans to give you the future you (and your grandchildren) hope for."* (Jeremiah 29:11 MSG)

There is a good work for you to do. There is a good work for your grandchildren to do. It was created in Christ Jesus and prepared in advance for you to do by our heavenly Father. God has an incredible story, and he has taken a piece of it and has placed it in your hearts.

You can help your grandchildren answer the questions of life when you first answer them for yourself.

Your Commitment

I will commit to make a concerted effort to help my grandchildren answer these questions of life for themselves.
I know I have to answer them for myself.
I will search my heart and endeavor to have a genuine relationship with God through Jesus Christ.

Reflections

- What is keeping you from discovering who you really are?

- What is keeping you from building a relationship with Jesus Christ?

- What eternal purpose were you created for?

- What kind of legacy are you intentionally leaving?

*Dear Heavenly Father, thank you for understanding me before
I was born and for establishing a plan and purpose for my life.
Thank you that you created me in your image. Please do your
work in and through me. I give my life totally over to you!
You are my God and Lord.
Amen!*

Real-Life
From a loving Grandson

My grandfather was a gentle man who loved Jesus. From my earliest remembrance he had a harmonica in his pocket and a song of praise in his heart. I recall most evenings the hymns of faith would ring out for the entire house to hear. At times he was playing, others he was just singing at the top of his lungs. If a hymn had five verses he sang or played them all.

In his rural church he would often stand and lead worship with his harmonica in hand as there was no one to play the piano. When he sang and led worship with those precious believers, he would bellow out the unashamed strains of all the old familiar songs of the faith. He was a worshipper before he was a farmer, father, husband or grandfather. His love for Jesus, his commitment to be a man of worship, modeled for me the heart of a man of God. On my old roll top desk is a picture of me as a toddler sitting on Grandpa's knee as he played his harmonic for me, as he did for all of his grandkids.

I am my grandpa's legacy. He instilled in me the heart of a

worshipper and today my greatest joy is leading my family in worship, whether around our old piano or like he did singing out for all to hear unashamed strains of the precious songs of the faith in the gathering of the faithful.

Thanks grandpa, I owe you a great debt, one for which you have been repaid, over and over again over the 26years since you have been at Jesus side. I love you as much today as I did back then perched upon your steady knee. My love and gratitude grows with each passing day.

– Daniel

Chapter 10
First Things First

The distance between you and your grandchildren is the distance between you and the love of God. Show your grandchildren first how to love and honor Jesus Christ.

Fall in love with Jesus,
and your grandchildren
will fall in love with the Jesus in you.

Love God

The Apostle Paul gives you the solution to being a grandfather; you will be known by your love. In I Corinthians 13 he tells you how. *"Love is patient, love is kind. It does not envy. It is not self-seeking. It is not easily angered. It keeps no record of wrongs. Love does not delight in evil but rejoices with the truth. It always protects al-*

ways trusts, always hopes, and always perseveres. This love never fails." (I Corinthians 13:4-8a)

A few years ago my wife made a comment to me that really shook me to the core. She said, "I know you love me, but are you in love with me?" I realized then and still do that our love is so imperfect. We use the same word, "love" for loving our cars, sport's team or pizza. I know the love we have for pizza would never be compared to the love we have for our wives, kids or grandchildren. We still need the kind of love God offers to us.

We know our love is so far from what Paul described. The Apostle goes on to write, "When that which is perfect (God's love) has come, then that which is in part (our love) will be done away." (I Corinthians 13:10 NKJ) Since that is true for all of us he goes on and says, "Pursue love..." (14:1a)

Perfect means complete – lacking nothing – fully mature. God, as displayed by Jesus Christ, is the only source of this perfect, mature, lacking-nothing love. I know I am not and will never be perfect in this world. If you don't believe me, ask my wife.

When you pursue God's perfect, mature love in your own life you can't help but pass it onto your own family.

This perfect love is demonstrated to us by our loving Heavenly Father. *"For God so loved the world (you) that he gave his one and only son, that whosoever believes in him will have everlasting life. For God did not send his Son into the world to condemn the world, but to save the world through him."* (John 3:16, 17)

A lot of people think God is mad at them. They think He has to be because of how messed up their life is.

God is not mad at us;
He is mad for us;
He is mad about us.

Because of God's love, Jesus Christ, God's only Son, died on a cross, and was raised from the dead to put the world right again. God LOL - Loved Out Loud!

It does not matter about your past, pain or sin. God forgives you and offers you his love and a brand-new start. All you have to do is receive him. This is the love we need and the love each of our grandchildren needs.

If you need to receive Christ for the first time or rededicate your life to Christ you can do so right now. Pray this prayer with me:

"Thank you God for sending your only Son, Jesus Christ, to die on a cross and pay my debt. Show me how much you love me. Please come into my life and make me the man you want me to be. Thank you for giving me your love found in Jesus Christ. May this love be shown through every part of my life! Amen

You can't give your grandchildren
what you have not first received for yourself.
So pursue God's love.

Live for God

If God can become man,
then he can do anything in
and through you as a grandfather.

You can unlock God's love only by committing to live a life that echoes now and for eternity. I have said before that so many people, including grandfathers, are making a living but not living a life that demands an explanation.

A life without God in the center is no life at all.

We have a tendency to commit to a lot of things that in view of eternity matter little. When we commit to living for God both in our lives and in our relationships, it matters for now and for eternity. I said this earlier in the book, but it is worth repeating.

What you want your family and your grandchildren
to say about you after you are gone
is written with the pen of your life.

More importantly, what do you want God to say about you when you meet Him on the other side? I know what I want Him to say to me.

You are my son whom I love
and in whom I am well pleased.
You were my good and faithful servant.
He writes these words with the pen of my life.

Begin to live and love the way God desires for you. Fall in love with God through Jesus Christ, and He will become the true love of your life. Your family and grandchildren will love the change.

You may become the only Jesus your grandchildren ever meet.
You can't give them what you have not first received for yourself!

Live to Leave a Legacy for God

The worth of the life you live as a grandfather
will be measured most by the legacy you live.

Over the many years that I have been a grandfather, I have not been a perfect man. I have gotten angry, argued with my wife in front of grandchildren (that is a no, no), hurt feelings and received appropriate correction for my attitude and behavior from both my wife and my daughter. But with all my faults I have always and continue to say I am sorry and have asked God and others to forgive me.

I don't know why I am bringing this up, but I really do believe that admitting wrong and asking for forgiveness is at the heart of the gospel. It is the true beginning of living and eventually leaving a Godly legacy. Admitting a need for a Savior in the present is the true beginning of eternal life for me and my grandchildren.

It is a life that is worth living and leaving.
Let it all go and imagine the possibilities!

The word "legacy" can define what people say about me after I am gone. Fair enough? I will not be defined by the stuff I hold onto but by the life I give away. That is how we define the life of Christ. He freely gave His life away that we could have eternal life. How about you?

My dad was one of those guys. I asked him once when I was a young man why he decided to sell everything we had and move us all onto a mission field. At that time I thought he was the dumbest man on earth.

It is amazing that as I got older my dad got so much smarter.

He finally told me, "Dan, your mom and I made a decision many years ago that there was nothing we owned that was worth taking with us, so we sent it all ahead." My dad is in heaven enjoying his investments.

> *What kind of investments are you making now*
> *that you will enjoy for eternity?*
> *Give it all away and imagine the possibilities!*

Your Commitment

I will not just talk about my faith but will intentionally commit to demonstrate my love for God and Jesus Christ. I won't just talk a good game, but I will choose to walk my talk by seeking to be the spiritual patriarch in my family. I will never be able to be the grandfather God wants me to be without first receiving and then giving God's unfailing love.

Reflections

- Where are you in your relationship with Jesus Christ?

- If you died tonight would you go to heaven? Would your children and grandchildren?

- How is your relationship with God? Are you a church-goer or a committed follower of Jesus Christ?

- What is coming first in your life? People or things?

- What is keeping you from saying, "I am sorry, please forgive me!"

- How are your eternal investments?

- What are you hanging onto that has little eternal significance?

Prayer of Commitment

Dear Heavenly Father, thank you for sending your only Son, Jesus Christ, to die on a cross and pay for my sin and show me how much you love me. Please come into my life and make me the man you want me to be. Thank you for giving me your love found in Jesus Christ. May this love be shown through every part of my life!
Amen.

Real-Life
From a loving Granddaughter

I was fortunate enough to have my grandparents invite me into their home where they comforted and supported me through the most difficult time of my life. I will never be able to show or express just how much I appreciated them for always being there for me. During that time my relationship with my grandfather grew to be very close. He has been one of the most influential men in my life. My grandfather has taught me values, beliefs and a work ethic that I will uphold and pass down to my own children.

Prior to living with him I had faith in God, but he showed me what it means to have a relationship with God. He participated in my baptism which was the most powerful experience of my life. He has shown me through his actions the importance of family, faith, generosity and love. He has been a blessing to me and our entire family. I thank God every day for him and so proud to call him grandpa.

– Ashley

Conclusion

Scripture says that without a vision the people, your grandchildren, will perish. Another version says that without a vision the people, your grandchildren, will stumble all over themselves, because they do not know where they are going.

Reminder: If you don't know where you are going,
any road will take you there.

Don't give up! You can live and leave a legacy that will help your grandchildren change and serve their world. Only God knows the ultimate end. I don't know about you, but I want to become part of their destiny. How about you?

Expressions of Appreciation

I would hope my grandchildren would say these things about me if they were asked.

- He talks and listens to me.
- He tells me how much he loves me.
- He is patient with me.
- He treats my parents well.
- He's nice to my friends.
- He invites me to go and do things with him.
- He disciplines me only when I deserve it.
- He isn't afraid to admit when he is wrong.

- He prays for me.
- He loves and serves God with all of his heart, soul, mind and strength.

Closing Commitment

You really can become a grandfather whose life demands an explanation.

Choose not to blend in.
Choose to stand out.

You really can become a grandfather who stands out and doesn't just blend in.

If you want to become great in the eyes of your grandchildren,
try descending, become a servant
and you will find genuine greatness.

You really can become a grandfather who leaves a legacy that echoes now and for eternity.

Do not fear failure;
Fear you would spend your life
succeeding at what does not matter.

Closing Reflection

What kind of legacy do you want to leave for your grandchildren?

My dad had served among the Native Americans as a missionary for over 38 years. Most of his grandchildren did not know him well but when he passed away they honored those years with love and respect. My dad could never keep the left bottom of his dress shirts tucked in. So at his memorial service the grandsons wore it out the same way he did. It became a tribute to a legacy worth living and remembering.

Remember, today is the beginning of the rest of your life;
go live the one God wants!

What or who is keeping you from living out that legacy?

If you can't see it, you will not believe it and
if you can't believe it, you will not live it!

Critical Question

If you had unlimited resources and complete freedom to fail what would you attempt as a grandfather?

Doing what is best has never been a provision issue.
It is either a seeing or a believing issue.

Concluding Prayer

My Heavenly Father, thank you for the children and grandchildren you have given me to love and cherish. Help me become the man that both lives and leaves a legacy that pleases you and stirs up my grandchildren to love and good deeds. I am not that man yet but I will commit my life to be that man. I will continue to trust and obey you. God give me eyes to see and a heart that believes. It is only then that I will be able to imagine your possibilities! Amen!

Real-Life Grandfathering

One generation shall praise your works to another, and shall declare your mighty acts. Psalm 145:4 Grandchildren are the little footsteps that connect generations: if I would have known how wonderful it would be to have grandkids, I would have had them first....

News Flash! You really do not have to do very much to become a good grandparent; can you roll around on the floor under a make-believe blanket tent, share a funny story, offer a front door hug, put a diaper on right side up, set up a backyard pool with a hose and a sprinkler, give and endless "horsey ride" or sit through hours of Sponge Bob while feasting on that long hidden can of SpaghettiOs?

One of my bravest grandsons always tells me, "Papa you are the oldest person in the world"; correct! After two hours with him...I believe it too!

We hear it all the time, "there has got to be more than this", everyone is looking for a brighter, easier, more encouraging way to get through their day. So many grandfathers have come and gone their faces fading overtime, but those memories become our treasures. The one memory that will last for generation is the warming joy I feel deep inside when my grandkids are squeezing my hands.

– Bill

When God created all His creation He said it was good;
But when He created grandchildren in His image
He said they were not just good,
they were very good; excellent in every way.
They really are the "Yes of God."
And so are you.

Dedication

I dedicate this book to my grandchildren. You inspire me to be the kind of grandfather I can become, because you deserve God's best. I commit to leave you a Godly legacy, one that will enrich your lives now and echo through eternity, because you are my grandchildren whom I love and in whom I am well pleased.

Gabby – You are so beautiful, creative and smart. You must take after your mother. I have never forgotten those precious times at our favorite bagel shop. Thanks for showing me how much God loves me. God wants to use your incredible creativity and channel it for other's good. When you see beauty and creativity, I pray it inspires not only your art and stories but also greater insight into the God who made it all and made you too! God told me to tell you that you really are his best; now go and be who you are!

Kayla – I love our talks and hearing you laugh. It is an honor to watch you grow into the woman God has destined you to become. You are not just beautiful but joyful and full of life. Don't let time, circumstances or others ever take that from you. Your life reveals your caring spirit and your laughter shows a joy in your heart. Your love for others is expressed in both your smile and your tears. I pray God will turn your tenderness and joy into the seeds of destiny for you and for those who have the privilege of knowing you. You know what is really cool? God likes to laugh, love and weep just like you.

Alex – What a man you are becoming. I love to walk, talk and work with you. I see a lot of Christ in you, because you truly have a servant's spirit. I love your boyish energy, friendliness and kindness. I think you have never met a boy or girl you do not try to like. You truly are your Heavenly Father's son! May God continue to nurture his loving and caring spirit in you. He wants to use you to serve those who are hurting and in need. I think God is smiling even now, because he sees who you can become. It is my job to help bring it out of you!

Dylan – You have not seen anything yet! Life is just beginning to reveal what's in your mind and in your heart. I love your curiosity, nerdy-ness and willingness to learn. You remind me of a human video game ("Love iPad") full of amusement, functions and possibilities. I think you take after your dad. I love hearing your laughter as the "The Claw" finds those places of sensitivity and joy. I know God has great hopes for you; he sees an incredible destiny in you. Only time, life and eternity will reveal all that is in the heart of God for you. Seek him with all your heart, and you will find your true delight, purpose and potential. That will be truly fun to see; I will bring the "The Claw!"

Bella – What a gorgeous lady you are becoming with your blonde hair, blue eyes and energetic personality. You remind me of your Grandma! I love listening to you sing at the dinner table, on the couch, in your bed, in the car and especially in my heart. I think someday God is going to turn all of his love, joy and melody and sing it to the world through your life. Don't let anyone silence the song God has placed in your heart. Sing, girl, sing! God, Grandma and I are singing along with tears of joy!

Hallie – Thank you so much for your hugs - my knees love them. You too are becoming an elegant example of what a lady should become with your pretty hair, ballet shoes and stylish apparel. What can I say? You raise the joy level of the whole family. I think when God sees you in your innocence and virtue, he must smile and say, "That is my girl in whom I love and in whom I delight!" You really bring a smile to my face every time I see you, especially when you say, "I love you, Papa!" Thanks for the memories, God and I love you too!

Danny – My namesake! What can I say other than the number seven really is an excellent number? Your name means, "God is my judge." May God judge you someday to be a man with a godly heart. May your energy and enthusiasm be channeled to make a difference in your world, whether a fireman, counselor or pastor. Make your dad proud as he has made me proud! Remember to always love and honor your Grandpa, because I have pictures.

Meet Dr. Dan Erickson

Dan Erickson practices what he preaches. He learned the principles in this book not only from intently studying scripture but also from trying to be the best grandfather he can be to his seven grandchildren – Gabby, Kayla, Alex, Dylan, Bella, Hallie and Danny.

At the same time, he strives to be a loving husband to his wife, Cathy, and father to his children, Shannon and Doug. Dan and Cathy have been partners – in life and in ministry – for more than four decades.

Dan and Cathy are the founders of People Matter Ministries. They speak, lead and live out of the personal commitment forged by the Scriptures and real-world experiences. They are driven by the conviction that people really matter most to God.

Dr. Dan has a bachelor's, a master's and a doctoral degree in ministry. Dan has in-depth leadership experience, including executive and pastoral positions in four dynamic churches. He also served as the executive vice president of Northwest Graduate School Doctor of Ministry program and as national director of denominational and parachurch relations with Promise Keepers.

Dan also provided leadership as executive director for the National Coalition of Men's Ministries as well as serving as Chief Servant Leader of People Matter Ministries. Cathy has founded ministries to single moms, their families and for victims of natural disasters.

Additional Resources*
by Dr. Dan and Cathy Erickson

Finding Your Greater Yes

Finding Your Greater Yes Study Guide

God Loves Do-Overs

God Loves Do-Overs Study Guide

Why Ministry to Men?

Imagine the Possibilities!
Devotional

Imagine the Possibilities!
Facing the Challenges in Life
Devotional

An Unstoppable Force
A Christian Manifesto

Maximize Your Marriage
CD set with notes

*Find these and other helpful resources at
www.peoplematterministries.com.

About People Matter Ministries

Purpose...

"To help people discover, develop and deploy their finger-print of potential."

> *"There are no ordinary people."*
> – CS Lewis

We believe...

- People are created in the image of God with dignity and worth.
- People are God's and Mankind's most valuable resource.
- People are individuals who are "Uniquely You."
- People can discover, develop and deploy their own "Finger-print of Potential."
- People discover and develop their greatest potential in the context of a safe and trusting environment.
- People are best served and deployed when led by "Servant Leaders."

Through responsible leadership we will ...

- Honor God in all we do and say.
- Provide motivation with vision and purpose.
- Provide expertise with a commitment to integrity and service.
- Promote and celebrate uniqueness and diversity.
- Be careful listeners, faithful stewards and consistent example.

"My greatest fear is not failure.
It is succeeding at something that does not matter."
-New Tribes Missionary, Author Unknown

General Information:

Mailing Address:
People Matter Ministries
PO Box 476
Lee's Summit, MO 64086

Website: www.peoplematterministries.com
Office Phone: 816.877.3663
Mobile: Dr. Dan Erickson – 816.679.7058
Email: Derickson@peoplematterministries.com